What About Me?

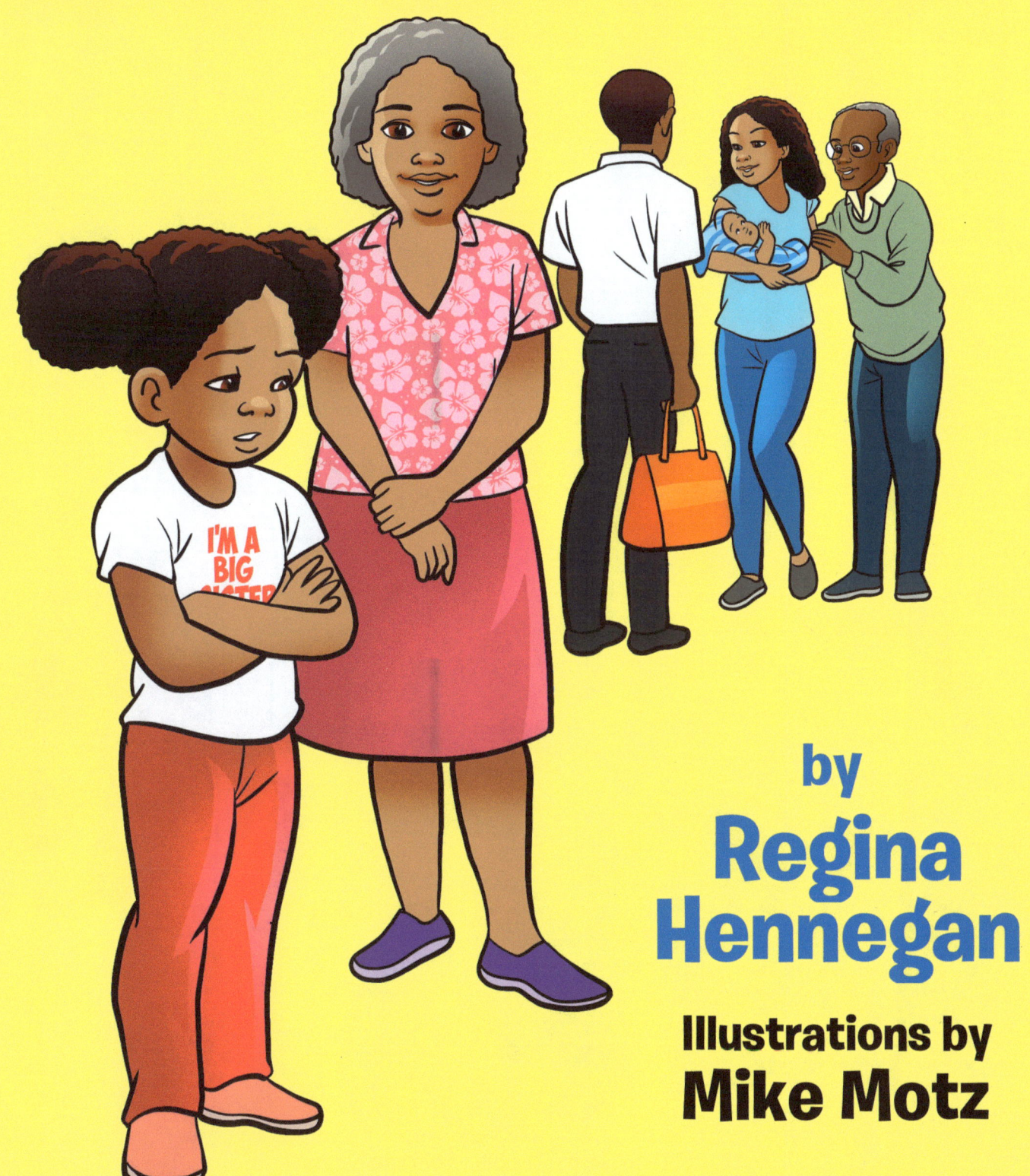

by
Regina Hennegan

Illustrations by
Mike Motz

What About Me? © 2021 Regina Hennegan.
All Rights reserved. No part of this publication may be reproduced or transmitted
in any form or by any means, electronic, mechanical, including photocopy,
recording, or any information storage and retrieval system,
without permission in writing from the author.

I dedicate this book to the loving memory
of my amazing father who always encouraged me
to follow my dreams and to make sure my books
were published for the world to read.

To my beautiful, strong, and courageous mother
who showed me through her faith and strength
that I can do all things through
Christ that strengthens me.

To my children, my grandchildren, and my husband.
You all are my biggest supporters.

My siblings, my nieces, and my nephews.
I love you all, and may my books
forever be a part of our family
for generations and generations to come.

Today's a really special day.
My baby brother's coming home.
But if this day's so special,
Then why do I feel alone?

Everyone is so happy.
They kiss and hug him tight.
My grandma looks at me and says,
"Sweetie, is everything alright?"

Oh, Grams, ever since the baby came,
No one seems to notice me.
It's like Mom, Dad, you, and Grandpa
Are the only ones he sees.

What happened to my story time
when we would cuddle with my bear?

And all the silly times when Daddy tried to braid my hair.

And Grandma, what about the time
you took me to the store
And I got to pick whatever I wanted.
Remember? That's when I turned 4.

Oh, Grandma, what will become of me
Now that the baby's finally home?
Will I get my mommy and daddy back?
Or will I always feel alone?

Oh, sweetie, I do understand
why you feel this way.
Your mommy also felt this way about her sister.
She didn't want her to stay.

But just because the baby's here,
you shouldn't feel alone.
You see, your baby brother
is now part of your happy home.

You can help with feeding, changing, and cuddling with him too.

And you can still do all the fun things with your mom and dad that you love to do,

Now you have a little brother who will always look up to you.

There are so many fun things you can teach him to do.

Like to tie his shoe?

Fly a kite?

And even ride a bike?

Wow! I think I'm going to like being a big sister now.

Yes, Grandma, everything is alright.

About the Author

My name Is Regina Hennegan. I am an author and educator, director and owner of my in-home daycare for over 24 years. A native of Buffalo New York, born and raised in this city. A wife and a mother of 5 beautiful children, a grandmother of two beautiful grandchildren. Reading was always my passion. Coming from a large family, reading took me away to a place of quietness, peace, and serenity.

As I became older I realized that I had a gift of writing. As a child I began writing poems and would hang them on my bedroom wall for display for everyone to see, and when my friends would read them they would say, "Girl, you write so beautifully." I began my journey writing children's books when my son was born 20 years ago. I published my first children's book in 2017 titled *Oh My Gosh! There's a Mouse in My House*, and now I am blessed to have my second book published and titled *What About Me?*

I give all praises to God for blessing me with this gift of writing and allowing me to share it with so many children. I pray that each book will bring laughter and love to everyone who reads it.